Song of the Seven Herbs

**by
Walking Night Bear
and
Stan Padilla, illustrator**

Also available: Cassette tape of **Song of the Seven Herbs**
Full-color prints of selected illustrations, suitable for framing.

For full details, write: Gold Circle Productions
P.O. Box 586
Nevada City, CA 95959

Library of Congress Cataloging in Publication Data

Walking Night Bear.
        Song of the seven herbs.

        Summary: Seven tales based on North American Indian lore relate how the Creator gave us herbs and why we are
to be thankful for them.
        1. Indians of North America—Legends.
        2. Indians of North America—Ethnobotany—Juvenile literature.
        3. Herbs—Folklore—Juvenile literature.
        1. Indians of North America—Legends.
        2. Indians of North America—Ethnobotany.
        3. Herbs (in religion, folklore, etc.)
I. Padilla, Stan, 1945-   , ill. II. Title
E98.F6W253 1987 398.2 42 08997 87-10234

ISBN 0-913990-56-6   90 10 9 8 7 6 5 4 3 2

Published in the United States of America by Book Publishing Company, Summertown, Tennessee.
Typesetting by Typecraft Company, Nashville, Tennessee.
Printed in the United States of America by R.R. Donnelley & Sons Company.

Contents

This book
is respectfully dedicated
to the spiritual sources of the Sky World
for their guidance and inspiration,
and to the children of the world:
May you always keep the light shining in your eyes,
and share these stories with future generations.

Introduction

These stories come to us from the Sky World. They are like seeds which grow from deep roots to reach again towards the sky. Given to us for a purpose, these stories are meant to be.

They were first planted in the mind of Walking Night Bear, who formed and cared for them. Through his inner thoughts and prayers they sprouted and strengthened.

He shared them with me, and I was able to give them color and brilliance from flower to root.

Each plant has its own story and teaching, but each lives together in a wholeness with the others. They can lead us on a pathway back to the Earth, and back to the stars.

These stories belong to us all, so carry them with love and respect.

Stan Padilla

We Give Thanks

Creator of All Good Things,
We give thanks to you for making our world so beautiful.
We give thanks to you,
    sacred Four Directions,
    sacred Four Winds,
    sacred Mother Earth,
    Sky World and Star Nations.
We give thanks to you all for bringing the plant down to us.
We thank you
    for the beauty of the plant,
    for the strength of its healing,
    for the goodness of its color,
    for the strength of its smell,
    and the cleanness of its spirit.
We give thanks to you, Mother Earth,
    for taking care of the plant,
    for giving it a home to grow in,
    for the strength you provide,
    for your warmth,
    and for your protection.
We give thanks to you, Grandfather of the Four Winds,
    for bringing the sacred air of movement, and
    for the messages of the Four Directions,
    so that the plant may grow and be a brother and sister
    to all living beings.
We give thanks to you, Grandfather in the Clouds,
    who brings the rain to our brother the plant.
We give thanks to you, Grandfather of the Lightning,
    for your cleansing.

We give thanks to you, Grandfather of the Thunder,
    for your blessing.
We give thanks to you, Sun,
    for your warmth,
    for your strength of light,
    for your strength of growth.
We give thanks to you, Moon, for being gentle in the night.
We give thanks to you, all good forces of healing,
    for your work in the plant,
    for the little people who weave the spirit above
    and beneath the earth.
We give thanks to you, sister plant,
    for your patience,
    for giving us the strength in the body and spirit.
Thank you for being there!
We ask for your forgiveness
    whenever we misuse you,
    whenever we don't honor you,
    whenever we don't appreciate you,
    whenever we forget to say "thank you."
We give thanks to you, brother plant,
    for your patience in being with us in the four seasons,
    for showing us the sacred circle of life.
We ask to learn from you, sister plant, patience
    and the love of light and life.
We ask you, Creator, to share with us the strength and
    beauty of the plant, that we may be filled with light
    and warmth, and in our hearts be at peace.
We ask Thee with all our relations.

HO

The Plant of Gold

When the Creator of All Good Things created the beautiful world, He made everything good! What a privilege it is for us to live on it!

The animals and man lived in harmony among the trees and the plants, the mountains and the water. Everything on Mother Earth lived in balance and in freedom. So all His creation was one good thing.

However, as you all know, we not only have "the Creator of Good Things," there is also someone we could name "the Creator of All Bad Things."

When the Creator of Bad Things looked at all this peace and harmony, his mind was no longer at rest. He spent a lot of time thinking and looking for ways to bring his share of darkness into the world.

It is not as easy as you think. When everything is in harmony and balance, it is very difficult to disturb it. Because the Creator of Bad Things was not at rest anymore, he created hatred, greed, and jealousy, and put these onto the people living in the creation of good.

11

Of course, he could not reach everyone. Still, a great many people had his help and the strength to bring all the bad things to other people, and to our brothers and sisters in the animal kingdom.

Soon many of the people and animals started to get sick in the spirit, and in the blood, and very soon in the whole body. The blood began to lose its red color, the stomachs got sick, and the people felt so tired. Then the balance, peace, and happiness started to leave the good work of the Creator of All Good Things.

When our Good Creator saw what had happened, He was very unhappy. Then He thought of an action of His own to help the poor people and the animals. He created the first herb, a plant to help the suffering on Mother Earth.

He took the plant to the Sun and asked her for her help. She is so generous, that she gave her light and strength to the plant. Then He went to the Moon, and the Moon gave his peace and love to it. After that, He travelled to the stars, who gave their harmony and strength to the plant.

He then asked Mother Earth if she would be so kind as to give the herb the strength of growth. The Winds, the Rains, the Thunder, and the Lightning also gave their help.

Mother Earth accepted the herb with thanks because, when her children suffer, she is suffering too.

What a beautiful and lovely plant this herb was. It looked like real gold! It had the most beautiful light radiating out of it. Out of love for the people and the animals, the herb helped them get strong again in the blood, in the body, and in the spirit.

Everyone who felt sick from the bad medicine of the Creator of Bad Things went to the plant for healing. Everyone was so happy, especially the beautiful herb, because she loved to help so much.

After a while the plant was used so much that she became hard to find. There was a reason fo this! Both the people and the animals went after the plant whether they needed it or not. Not only this, most of them did not say "thank you" to either the plant or the Creator of Good Things. They forgot to say "thank you" to the Mother Earth, too, and to the Sunshine and the Rain. Everyone took it for granted that the plant would help them all of the time.

First the plant was very sad about it, and then because she gave of herself so much, she herself got weaker and weaker. It was sad to watch the poor plant getting more and more scarce and weak.

At last the herb didn't know what to do anymore, and she called out to the Creator of All Good Things for help. The Creator of All Good Things heard the sad story and He wept with the plant.

The Creator then spoke to the plant, "All I wanted to do was to help the sick people and animals with the love I have for them. There are few who say "thank you" to you, my healing herb, and to Me, and to all the ones who have given the gift of strength to you."

As the Creator continued to think about it, He not only got sad but angry, and after a while He told the herb, "All the ones who need your help will have to learn a lesson. From now on I will not make it easy for them!" said the Creator.

He changed the golden color of the herb to green. Then He took away the smoothness of the leaves and stem and put tiny little hairs on them. These hairs He filled with little lightnings, each one of them! Then the Good Creator spoke again.

"Anyone who needs your help will have to suffer first, because they have not been thankful to you. The sting they suffer will remind them that they have not said the sacred word. But I will not be too hard on them. All the strong and healing powers you have, I will leave you," said the Creator.

So it was that, from that day on, we call this special herb the "Stinging Nettle."

If by chance you should get stung by this herb, don't get angry with her. It is not her fault. Say "thank you" to her. For even the pain gives healing to you, because it reminds you to say "thank you" to the plants, the Good Creator, the Mother Earth, the Sun, the Moon, and the Rain, and also the Thunder and the Lightning.

There is a secret I would like to share with all of you. When you remember to say "thank you," in time the Stinging Nettle will not sting you anymore! You will find out for yourself.

Remember, she still has the same great healing power she had when she was not green and stinging. She is, in her heart and spirit, still a plant of pure gold.

Todzi-touega

I would like to tell you a story about a plant the Peyote people call Todzi-touega. Isn't it wonderful? Listen to the sound of it: tod′-zee too-ay′-guh.

A long time ago there lived a big family of Indians who dwelt in a dry and hot part of the country which today we call California. These Indians were very good children of the Creator because they lived together in peace and love. There was no need to make war dances because they were a people of peace.

Each day they would give thanks to the Creator, the Mother Earth, and all the Good Spirits. When they had to kill an animal or plant for food, they would bring offerings and thanks.

Life was good to them. In fact, it was so good to them that the Old Medicine Man did not have to spend much time healing them. He could spend his time giving ceremonies and special offerings to all good things above Mother Earth, beneath Her, and all that lived on Her.

17

This Old Medicine Man had a grandson. His name was Climbing Bear. He was learning from his Grandfather and was helping him; and he did it all with great love and joy in his heart. He gave his Grandfather and all the old people the respect they deserved.

However, as you probably know, when all things are good, there is someone who cannot be at peace. Not far from where little Climbing Bear lived there was a Medicine Man who was just the opposite from his Grandfather. This other Medicine Man would only let bad things come out of his heart.

I am sure you understand that he was very unhappy to see all the people living in harmony. So, one very dark night he took his bag, which was filled with bad medicine, and went very quietly to the water spring in the mountains. This was the very spring of water that helped quench the thirst of the people, the animals, and the plants where Climbing Bear lived. He poisoned this water with his bad medicine, and soon it started to affect both the people and the animals.

Their stomachs started to cramp up, food gave them pain, and by the end of the day everyone was sick. The hunters could not go hunting. The women could not cook food. The animals got so weak that even the strong horse could not bear to have anyone ride him.

Climbing Bear's Grandfather, due to his old age, was the one who suffered most. He was so weak that he had to lie down for good. He called his grandson and spoke to him.

"My son, I am too weak to help our people and the animals. They are all going to die unless they can get the right medicine. Go up to the hills in the North and make the offering I have taught you. Then bring the herb so we can make a medicine for the people and the animals. Then they will all be well again."

He then described the herb so that Climbing Bear could find it.

"I know you are still very young, but you will find the plant with the help of the Good Spirit," his Grandfather said, comforting him.

So off went Climbing Bear to the hills, although he could only walk slowly because he was very sick. When he reached the hills in the North, the Grandfather of the West had already taken the sun to sleep. Climbing Bear had just enough time to say the evening prayer, and all was dark.

"How can I find the healing herb when it is dark?" he said to himself. "If I wait till the morning light, many of my people and animals will already have died." He was especially worried about his Grandfather.

First he thought of waiting for the Moon, but then he realized that the Moon would not be shining brightly this night. He tried very hard, but he still could not find the plant in the darkness. He knelt down on Mother Earth and spoke to the Creator and asked for help. He knew in his heart that the Creator always helps when we ask in the right manner.

When he got up and looked around, it was still dark as before. He knew that the plant grew there because he remembered collecting some with his Grandfather. In despair he started to look on the ground for the herb, but he could not find it! In the darkness everything looked black!

He stood up again and raised his eyes to the sky of the night. The only lights he could see were the stars. Their light was not strong enough to light up the ground. Again he fell down to his knees with tears in his eyes, and called up to the stars.

"Please help me. You are the only ones with light in the dark night. Please help me to find the herb that will make my people and brother animals healthy again. Otherwise they will perish."

As he was calling out for help, he saw a Light Spirit coming to him and he heard a voice.

"We cannot make more light for you because we are so far away, but we are going to help you because you are a good child," said the Spirit.

As soon as the voice had spoken, he could see that from many stars in the sky a little light broke off. Soon all around him it was like a snowfall of little lights. They did not fall on the ground but settled down on the herb plant. All around him in the dark night was the light of the shining herb.

Little Climbing Bear knelt again to the ground and gave his full thanks to the Creator, the stars, the plant, and Mother Earth, and all the Good Spirits. Then he collected as much of the shining herb as he needed and went home to his people and animals with the last strength of his body.

His Grandfather was really happy and relieved when his grandson, Climbing Bear, returned with the herbs, and he saw they were the right ones! Although he had never seen the flowers that shined with the light of the stars, his grandson told him all about the wondrous experience.

Then the Old Medicine Man made the medicine tea and gave it to all the people and animals. Very soon everyone was happy and healthy again.

It is good for all of us that little Climbing Bear did not pick all the shining plants. If he had picked them all, there would be none left for us. So when you go out, even in the dark night, you will still be able to pick Todzi-touega because the little stars on it are still shining softly.

However, it is good to remember that most plants like to be picked in the daytime.

Do you know what the plant is called today? Most people call it "Yarrow."

Kosi, the Eagle,
and the Mountain Lion

Once upon a time there lived an Indian boy who was very special. Already as a small boy he had a very special gift in body and spirit. He was able to listen to what the people had to say. He listened to his Grandfather and Grandmother, and to the old people who spoke of the olden times and of the ways they lived and what they experienced.

He sat still and listened to all they had to tell. In his heart he did not question them or ask them silly things.

When he went out into Mother Nature with his father, he would be quiet and listen to all that his father had to tell him. When his mother was cooking food, or helping someone who was sick, man or animal, he would watch with an open mind, and he kept everything in his heart.

By the time he was a young man, he had a great knowledge about everything. He knew more than most people. One day he went to the Medicine Man and said to him, "I am a young man. I want to go up to the mountain and get my song and listen to what the Spirit has to tell me. Would you be so kind as to help me and tell me what to do? I ask you with all my love."

Tears of joy came to the eyes of the old, wise Medicine Man. He looked down at the young man. "You know so many things and yet you come to me for help. My Medicine tells me that you are someone special. I am so glad to help you."

So the old Medicine Man prepared him in the right old ways for his time in the mountains. Off the young man went into the mountains, leaving all food and other things at home.

It did not take him very long to find the right place in the mountains, because he let the Good Spirits lead him. After days of fasting and praying he got his power song. Soon a very special being from the Spirit World spoke to him. "You have been a good boy, and you are a good man. We have watched you from the World Above and are happy to see how well you have listened to the teachings of the people, and how you give thanks to everything. I tell you, you will be a very specially strong Medicine Man. We will help you and give you much power to help the people, especially the ones who are sick in mind and body."

With this the Spirit left the young man with a blessing. From then on the young man was called Kosi Agu, the "flower of the sun." We will call him as most people did, simply "Kosi."

While in the mountains, Kosi found two special friends: the Eagle, and the Mountain Lion. From that time on, wherever he was and wherever he travelled, these two friends followed him.

The Eagle would bring him messages from out of the sky, because Eagles can see everything. The Mountain Lion gave him strength of body, and protection, whenever he was in need.

Kosi got stronger day by day, not only in body, but also in knowledge and love. He loved everyone and helped whenever he could. He helped the sick people, the animals, the trees, and the water. Whoever needed his help, he would be there to give his best. So it was that he was loved and honored by everyone.

He lived a very simple life. He never tried to be more than he was. He knew that all that he did was a gift from the Good Ones in the Spirit World and our dear Mother Earth. He never forgot to say "thank you."

His special strength was that he knew all the herbs. He knew the time to pick and harvest them and how much to use. There was hardly any medicine growing on Mother Earth that he did not know.

Sometimes the Eagle would fly up to the top of the mountain and pick a special plant for him. When he did this, there was no need for Kosi to climb up the hill, and thus, he had more time to help the people. Sometimes a patient was very far gone and needed help quickly. The Eagle would fly where the herbs were and bring the medicine that Kosi needed to give. The Mountain Lion would help him dig up roots from the earth and help whenever there was a need.

These three worked very closely together and were the best of friends. All that they did, they did with good and great joy!

There was, however, one thing missing. Kosi was so busy helping all the people that he never had time to find a good wife for himself. So it was that he had no children of his own. And sad to say, there were no boys and girls who were like him when he was a boy who would listen and learn from him. Everyone behaved as though Kosi would always be there to help them.

As the years went by, Kosi's hair got as white as the snow. His face looked like the bark of a good old oak tree. Even the Eagle and the Mountain Lion were turning white with age. Only the medicine from Kosi gave them the strength to live.

One day in early spring, Kosi was lying on Mother Earth under a willow tree. He was listening to the singing of the birds, the wind, and the clouds. He was so happy. The Eagle and the Mountain Lion were at his side. All three were so happy in the beautiful springtime!

Suddenly they heard a loud sound, and a very strange Spirit Man from the mountain stood before them.

The Spirit Man said, "It is good to see you so happy. It is a good time. I bring good news to you. This evening you will all join us in the World Above. We all need you there, so prepare yourselves, and I will come when the sun sets in the evening." Then he departed with his song.

Kosi, the Eagle, and the Mountain Lion were very happy to go to rest in Mother Earth. Yet they had tears in their eyes because it was not easy to leave the Earth and all that they loved. They knew in their hearts that their years had brought them fullness, and their time upon the Earth was complete.

So Kosi sent a message to all the people and asked them to come to him, the Eagle, and the Mountain Lion. When they had gathered around in great numbers, Kosi said, "My dear friends, I and my brothers, the Eagle and the Mountain Lion, will leave this evening and go into the higher World Above. I would like to thank you for being so kind to us and loving us. We love you all so much, and it was with love and joy that we helped you all these years.

"We ask that you bury our bodies here in this meadow, sing songs to us, and respect this place where our bodies rest. I give you all my blessings."

As Kosi spoke to the people, they got very upset. They cried because they loved Kosi, the Eagle, and the Mountain Lion, so much.

After a while the Chief said, "Our dear Kosi, our dear Friends, you have been so good to us; we will never forget your love and care. Our children and grandchildren and all children to come will speak and sing great songs of you.

"We know your days are old and your spirits are looking forward to going up to the World Above. But one thing is worrying me and my people. Who is going to help us when you are gone? We do not know what herbs to use to make us well. We did not listen and learn from you. We just didn't think that you would leave one day and not be with us anymore. Can you not stay and teach us?"

As the Chief spoke these words, all the people, young and old, began to cry and ask Kosi for help. They wanted Kosi to teach them for just a little while longer.

Kosi got tears in his eyes, and so did the Eagle and the Mountain Lion. Kosi asked them to be quiet and give him time to think. He started to sing his strong power song and closed his eyes and spoke to the Great Spirit. After a while he opened his eyes and spoke.

"There is no time for teaching anymore, but the Great Spirit has given me the following message to comfort you. When our spirits have passed out of our bodies, you will bury us together here in the meadow. Soon you will find a plant growing in the meadow. The flower will be like my name and heart, the leaves like the teeth of my brother the Mountain Lion, and the roots like the legs of my friend the Eagle. This plant will help you to get stronger in body and spirit when you are sick. When there is no food, you can eat it and make tea out of it. Take it as a gift from me and my two friends."

Soon after Kosi had spoken, his spirit and the spirits of the Eagle and the Mountain Lion left their bodies. The three all had a smile of peace on their faces. The people buried them in the meadow with all the love and honor they deserved.

A few days later, after a good cleansing rain, the spring sun shone strong again, and all over the meadow grew a beautiful flower. It was not a tall plant. It was a flower like the radiating sun, with strong green leaves like the teeth of the Mountain Lion, and strong brown roots like the legs of the Eagle.

Soon the people discovered how right Kosi was. It helped the sick and fed their bodies, and most of the animals liked it too.

You will understand that from that time the plant is called by the name of "Kosi." We also call it "Dandelion" or "lion's tooth."

There are other names given to this plant too, but regardless of the name, you can always count on her to be healthy and good and healing as ever.

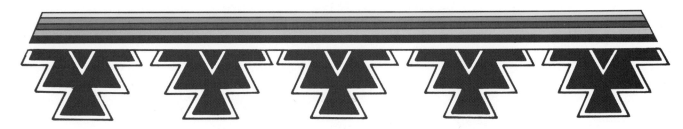

28

The Secret of Tomuni

There on Mother Earth stood the mighty Tomuni. He was a tall, strong mountain. His peak with a white cap of snow reached the blue sky. His feet and legs went deep down into Mother Earth. From the top of the mountain flowed a sparkling clear water that gave cooling to the thirsty ones, and to everything that was in need of it.

In the rocks lived the mountain goats, the mountain lions, the wild sheep, and so many other animals. In the trees sat the eagles and many birds.

Tomuni the Mountain was in harmony with his spirit and loved everything who lived there.

Deep inside of him was a very big cave where the Little People lived. They spent their time helping others, especially those who were sick. They helped the plants, and the animals, and the people. Although there are very few people who know about the Little People, and can see them, they are still very much alive, even today!

In the cave there was something very special. All over the walls were different crystals: white and clear ones, smokey colored ones, yellow and green ones. They gave strength and light and wisdom to the people and all those who lived nearby.

In one corner where the light could hardly reach, there was a crystal who was very little, but very beautiful. His color was deep purple, deeper than the sky above Tomuni. It was an amethyst crystal!

There he stood in the corner attached to the rock wall. Yet he was happy. That is where the Creator had put him, and that was good enough for him!

Often in the evening the Little People would light a special fire. The Mountain Spirit of Tomuni would come down, and he and the Little People would talk about many things in the Circle.

They would tell Tomuni about the people and animals they saw, and how they helped them, and what herbs they would give them. Tomuni would tell them of the sunshine, the rain, the sunrise, the sunset, and the beautiful things about the four seasons. So they would sit for hours and tell their stories, and the Little Amethyst could listen to it all.

Many, many years passed and every one was happy—or nearly everyone. After Little Amethyst had listened to all their stories, he had a growing wish in his heart, and this wish grew bigger and bigger as time went on.

He would say to himself, "Oh, if only I could see the Earth from the outside: the Sun, the Moon, the trees, the animals, and maybe even some people. Oh, how wonderful it would be if I could help them in some good way!" But it could not happen, because there he stood fast in the rocks and could not move.

The years went by and still his wish grew stronger and stronger. He felt he could also do something to help the sick and bring joy into the world.

One evening the Little People lit their special fire again, and this time one could sense from their mood that something sad was concerning them.

They called out to the Mountain Spirit Tomuni to come down and join them in the Circle. Then they all sat around the fire.

One old man from the Little People stood up and spoke to Tomuni and all the people in the Circle.

"Dear friends," the old man said softly, "today we are not here to share our joy. We gather here to ask for help. For hundreds of years we have been able to help the sick people and animals, and we could always find the right herbs for the Medicine Man. Often it was not very easy, but we always managed to help and could find the right herb."

"But now we are in trouble! The people out there on Mother Earth have started to form hard lumps in their bodies. The lumps look like pebbles in the river, some are big and some are small. They poison the blood and the spirit within them, and many of these people die, old ones, fathers, mothers, and even children. The suffering is great. We looked, but could not find any herbs or cure to help the sickness."

When he had spoken, all sat still and were thinking, and they all looked up to the Mountain Spirit of Tomuni.

After a long time Tomuni spoke and told them how much he was thinking of their problem and praying for them. Still he could not think of anything that would help.

Little Amethyst sitting on the rocks heard all of this, and in his heart he felt sad for these people. If only he could help, but how? Then he remembered that whenever someone does not know what to do anymore, there is always one who knows the right answer.

So it was he who prayed to the Great Spirit. "Please help me," said Little Amethyst, "I would like so much to help the people. I would do anything to help them!"

Now, as you all know, the Great Spirit listens to every prayer, even ones that come from small things like the Little Crystal.

Suddenly, a soft and beautiful light began to brighten the cave. The light became stronger and stronger and in the center stood the Good Creator.

He stood before the Little Amethyst and said, "For a long time I have known of your wish in your heart and I have listened to your prayers. It is very noble of you to want to help the people, but you will suffer greatly. Here you are safe and no danger comes to you, but out in the world it will not be easy for you. There is not only the sunshine, but there are the cold winds, and the snow, and many things you are not used to. Are you still willing to help?"

"Oh, Good Creator," said the Little Amethyst, "with joy in my heart I will help those who are sick. Please, Good Creator, let me help."

"So it shall be," said the Creator, "but I will have to change you a little before you go to the world outside."

34

He lifted the Little Amethyst softly from the rock and held him in his hands. Then he transformed him into a little green plant that had leaves like the shape of a heart.

Then he carried him out of the cave and through the mountains and into a little wood. There he planted him softly into the ground. It was springtime on Mother Earth, and with Her help the little plant grew well and soon had many children.

A few weeks later another little miracle happened. The most beautiful little flower, with a strong sweet smell, blossomed from the plant. It was the color of the Little Amethyst when he was a crystal in the mountains, a deep dark purple.

It did not take the Little People very long to tell the Medicine Man about the new plant, and tell him the story of the Little Amethyst. The Medicine Man was shown the little plant, and a big smile came to his eyes.

"Well, there is one problem for me," said the Medicine Man. "I cannot call you Amethyst like the crystal, but I would like to give you a name."

While he was thinking, he looked up to the sky just after the sun had set, and then a smile came to his eyes again, and he said to the little plant, "From now on your name shall be Violet, like the color of the Amethyst and the sky at sunset."

How happy the little plant was! Now he not only had a beautiful name, but he could also help the people to get well.

But the Good Creator was right, too. Even though the plant was full of love and kindness, it was not easy for him to live on Mother Earth.

When the sun was too strong, it had to hide its flowers inside the leaves because it was not used to so much light. So often the children who played in the woods and meadows did not see it, and trampled it down with their feet.

Of course, this hurt the Little Violet, but he was so full of love, and his will to help others so great, that he always bloomed anew again from very early spring to autumn.

If you ask any good person who knows this healing plant, he will sit down with you and light a special fire like the Little People. But watch the time! Because it will take him many hours to tell you of all the wonderful ways that the Little Violet can help cure people.

The Flowers from the Sky

There have always been times when people had to move to faraway places. Today it is easy to travel, but in olden times man had to travel by foot, or else his brother, the animal, helped carry him.

The time that this story took place was a long, long time ago. But as you see, not all forgotten. Why? You will soon find out!

It was a time when many new changes came about. There were wars among the people, and there were people who wanted more and more land that did not belong to them. They forgot that the Creator had provided plenty of land for everyone to live on in peace. There was enough land for food and hunting, and for a sacred place for offerings and prayers. There was even enough land left for the animals to live in their own freedom.

So it came to pass, that it was time for the tribe of good old Wanatu to leave its place of birth, death, and good life. There were the old ones, fathers, mothers, children and babies, and all the other people who belonged to the family of old Wanatu. He was the Chief and the Medicine Man.

First, they were quite lucky on their journey because there was enough game for food, plants and berries to eat, and plenty of water. So everyone kept strong, although in their hearts and spirits they were sad because they had to leave their beloved land.

However, all this began to change soon, and the land became more and more like the desert. There were very few animals to hunt or plants and berries to eat. The water was so scarce that it was hard to keep the thirst away.

The longer the journey went, the worse the situation became. First, the old ones, then the children, and then even the strong hunters became weaker by the day. Old Medicine Man Wanatu had great difficulty in finding any plants for eating and healing. There was only dry ground, and once in a while a dry bush of desert grass.

Tears came to his eyes when he saw the suffering of his people and animals. Great pain came to his heart when he saw how his people lost their courage and all their hope. Soon the time came when they could not move on any further. So they had to set up camp in the desert.

In the morning, Wanatu saw a little hill not far away to the West. He took his sacred Medicine Bag, and with the last strength left in his body he went up to the hill. There he gave offerings to the Great Spirit, and sang his power song.

Then he spoke to the Creator and asked for help for his people and animals. When he was finished, he sat down on the hill and wept tears of sadness and tears of joy because he knew that the Creator of All Good Things always helps when one asks in the proper manner and out of great need.

As he sat there, a mighty, old and wise Eagle came down from the sky and sat at his left side.

"The Good Spirits have heard your prayers," said the Eagle. "Have courage! Tomorrow morning you will find all over the land a plant that will feed you and your people and animals. You have to understand that it is very difficult to grow anything in dry and hot soil. It is a rough plant and nothing special to look at, but you can even use its roots." With this the Eagle spread out his wings and went up into the sky.

Wanatu rose early in the morning so he could greet the Sun as all good Indians did. As he walked out of his teepee, he saw all over the plain a strange plant.

The plants were three to four feet tall and the horses and other animals were eating them with great pleasure. The people who were up started to collect the leaves and roots as he told them to do. When he and others came back from thanking the Spirits and singing to the new day, they all had a good meal!

The plant was not sweet like honey, but bitter and tough. But it did not matter. It made them strong in the body, and everyone was thankful.

Well, their bodies were strong, but their spirits were not keeping up with their bodies. The people were sad in their hearts and minds. There was no hope left in their spirits and they felt very depressed. Joy, hope, and happiness left them.

When poor Wanatu saw this, he went back to the hills in the West. After he gave thanks for all the food and all the help, he gave an offering to the Spirits. Then he sang his Eagle song. He did not have to wait very long and the beautiful old Eagle came down to his side again.

He told the Eagle that hope and joy had left the spirit of his people. The old Eagle understood his worries because eagles are wise and know everything.

"I will help you," said the Eagle. "The one thing that will help you all is a piece of the sky. It will fill you with hope and happiness again."

Saying this, the Eagle spread his wings and flew up towards the blue sky. He picked small pieces out of the sky with his beak, and when he had landed on Mother Earth again, he put them on top of the plants that had grown overnight.

"In the morning all the plants will have flowers," said the Eagle. "Tell the women and children to pick them very, very carefully. They are very sensitive because the sky doesn't like to be touched too hard. Brew a tea out of the flowers and it will take away the sickness of no hope in the spirit."

So it was. In the morning all over the plain, blue flowers were on the plants!

The mothers and the children picked the flowers very, very carefully as Wanatu had told them. Soon they had collected enough. But they were also careful to leave some plants, blue and joyful, and shining back into the sky!

Then Wanatu made a tea as the Eagle had told him, and soon the spirit of hope and joy came back to them. They were all very happy and had courage again.

They made a big feast and sang songs of thanks to all who had helped: the Eagle, the plant, the flower, the good Mother Earth, and everyone.

With hope and joy in their hearts they soon found a beautiful land again. It was a good piece of Mother Earth, and She shared with them all that She had. Of course, many tears were shed over the memories of the old land, but everyone was thankful to have found a new home.

So, when you go over dry and warm ground and you find the wild Chicory flowers and wonder why they have the ends of their petals cut off, you will know why! It is because it was very difficult even for the Eagle to make a straight line or a rounded curve with his beak when he picked away a piece of the sky to help us.

Moonflower

A long, long time ago a girl lived with her parents, brothers, and sisters in a camp near the mountains. She was very beautiful and her heart was clean like the songs of spring. This was all given to her because she would always listen to her parents. When there was nothing special going on, she went to bed when the Moon started to lighten up the sky. And in the morning she would be there to greet the new day when the Sun rose in the East.

She had three things she loved very dearly. She loved the Moon, who gave her gentle quietness. She loved her friend, the Bear, who gave her love and wisdom. But most of all she loved the Rose, who gave her beauty.

As long as there were roses flowering, she would go in the morning and, with a friendly smile, ask the rose bush for one of his flowers. After saying "thank you" to him, she would place the rose flower in her long black hair. So it came that the people called her by the name of "Moonflower."

One day in late autumn when her brothers, the trees, stood in all their glory, and spread their beautiful colored leaves into the blue sky, her mother called her.

"Soon we will have the time of the cleansing of Mother Earth, and the frost and the cold will come with the snow from the North," said her Mother. "We have to be prepared for the winter. We have to have enough food for all of us for the coming three months. Your father and your brothers are out hunting for meat and hides.

"Please go out to the mountains to collect berries, and we will dry them for the months to come. Here are three baskets I have woven. Fill them up, but remember to leave enough for the animals and birds. Be careful. I hope you will be home soon. My prayers are with you."

With joy in her heart she called her friend the Bear and asked him if he would be so kind as to come along and help her. Moonflower knew that bears are especially good in finding spots where berries grow.

The Bear was only too happy to help his friend. So off they went through the forest towards the mountains. Once they were there, Moonflower, with the help of the Bear, found a good spot with lots of berries.

It did not take long and the first basket was full of blueberries. They put the full basket on a rock and left it there to be picked up on their way back home.

Off they went to the next place, a little farther away, but they did not notice that the Coyote was following them. They were just out of sight when the Coyote came out of his hiding place in the bush. With a big smile he ate all the berries in no time. Then he settled down in the sun and happily passed the time away with a full stomach!

After a while he followed Bear and Moonflower and found the next basket, and in no time finished that one too!

When Moonflower and the Bear had finished the third basket, it was getting late and the sun had started to go to sleep in the West. They both felt the day's hard work and were very tired.

When they came to collect the second basket, it was empty!

"Well," said Moonflower, "someone must have been very hungry."

After a while they came to the first basket, and they just could not believe their eyes when they saw that one was empty too!

"Well, that's too bad," said the Bear.

"Yes," said Moonflower, "I cannot go home with only one basket full of berries. Let's spend the night here, and fill them in the morning."

Soon the Bear found a little cave and they both settled down for a good sleep. In the morning they awoke early.

"I'm hungry," said Moonflower.

"So am I," said the Bear. "Come, let's eat the berries and we will find more a little further away from here."

But when they lifted the basket it was empty! The Coyote had eaten all those berries during the night.

The Bear sniffed the ground with his nose and angrily said, "It was the Coyote who has eaten all the berries. He has been following us. Today we have to be more careful. Let's go, we have a long day before us."

After they had their morning bath in the river and offered their prayers, off they went.

The Coyote left because he heard what the Bear had said, and he knew the Bear would give him a good whipping if he got hold of him. That would be one thing he would not enjoy at all!

But it was not a good day for Moonflower and the Bear. A thick fog settled in, and they could hardly see the berries; and what's more, they lost their way!

When the evening came, they did not even have the first basket full of berries. They hoped for a better day in the morning. The good Bear found another cave, and Moonflower lit a little fire. They ate the berries and some roots that the Bear had found, and went to sleep.

When they rose in the morning, the fog was gone, but instead of the sunshine everything was white. A heavy snowstorm had covered everything with snow, even the air.

They spent the day in the cave. It continued to snow for three more days and then things really got desperate for them. Moonflower felt very hungry and homesick. The Bear got anxious too, because it was time for his winter sleep.

The snow was three feet high. There were no berries to pick or roots to dig out of the ground to eat. And they did not know which way to go home.

In front of the cave grew many rose bushes, but now they had only bare branches; there were no flowers and no leaves.

Moonflower stood there before the rose bush and with tears in her eyes she said, "Oh, my dear rose bush, this is going to be the end of me. I am so hungry and cold. And it is also very hard for my friend the Bear. Is there no help for us?"

The rose bush thought for a long time, but he could not find a way to help. So he turned his prayers to Mother Earth. In a little while they heard a soft sweet sound coming from Earth, and suddenly the most beautiful woman appeared. In a warm and soft voice she said, "You two have always shown me love and respect. I will help you."

With these words she went to the rose bush and put the prettiest berries on it. They were a deep red. They looked like blood. They looked so good in the white snow.

"Let them stay on the bush for a little while so that the frost can make them ripe," said the woman. "The sun is not strong enough in the winter time to ripen them."

And away she went with her soft, yet powerful song.

After a while the rose bush told them that the berries were ripe. With great hunger Moonflower and the Bear started to eat them. They were most delicious! After they had eaten, they thanked the Mother Earth and the rose bush.

Then they filled all the baskets until they were full, yet there was plenty left for the birds and animals.

As all this was happening, it was not only Moonflower and the Bear who were having a hard time. Her mother and father and brothers and all the people in the camp were worried. They looked everywhere in the forest and mountains, but could not find them.

So it was that the Coyote found out what happened, and he felt sorry he had played such a bad trick on them. So he went off on his own to look for the two of them. It was just at the time that Mother Earth created the berries for the two. After a long time he found them.

"I am sorry to have led you into this," said the Coyote. "I know the way home and I would like to make it up to you by showing you the way."

Moonflower and the Bear were too soft-hearted to be mad at the Coyote anymore. They were happy to have his help.

"But before we go I would like to eat some of the berries," said the Coyote. "I am so hungry." And he went over to the rose bush.

The rose bush got very angry at the Coyote, so angry that his bark burst and out of it came thorns like cat claws. He scratched the Coyote all over. The Coyote cried out loud and fled the rose bush.

In a hurry he led them back to the camp. Everyone was happy and thanked the Creator and all the Good Spirits, especially Mother Earth, for their help.

As it turned out, the berries were most delicious. They are still good today if you just give the good frost time to make them ripe.

When you see a Coyote today, you can still see the scars on his pelt. You will never see him eating the berries of the rose bush.

Today the rose bush is still the most beautiful plant and has the most delicious berries. But from that day on he also has had the thorns. However, when you are very gentle with him, his thorns will not hurt you.

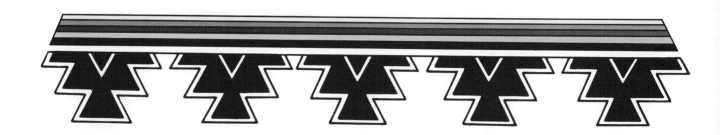

Bright Light

Children often listen to stories their Grandfathers and Grandmothers tell, and they wonder from where the stories come. When you ask the old people this question, they will say, "Well, my Grandmother or Grandfather told it to me."

Some of these stories came down to us from many, many generations, so far back in time that it is difficult to remember when or where.

The story I would like to tell you is one that goes back a long, long time. The people who lived on our Earth in those days had something in common with us today. They started to walk away from the Path of the Good Spirit and Light. The Creator, with all His fatherly love, tried very hard to bring them back to the right Path, but they would not listen to Him.

The Creator was very sad in His heart, but He had to teach the people a good lesson. So He took away the Sun and the blue of the sky, and He clouded the sky with thick, dark clouds. All the people and animals and everything on Mother Earth was covered with rain. And it rained, and rained, and rained!

This went on for a long, long time, and soon the only things showing were a few mountain tops. All other things were under water and drowned. Only a few people and animals and plants were left.

It was very sad, even for the Creator. But behind the dark clouds there was still the Sun. Although her light did not reach the Earth, the Sun could observe what was happening down there. It made her very sad because the Sun loves everything on Earth very much. But there was nothing she could do to help. She knew that the Good Creator had His reasons and knew exactly the right thing to do at the right time—even when it was not always easy to understand.

I am sure you all know that the Creator has many spirits to help Him with His good work. Some call them "Good Spirits," and others call them "Angels." Like the Creator, the Sun also has such helpers, because she would have a hard time doing all the good things she does alone.

One of the helpers, she called by the name of "Bright Light." She and the Sun were very close friends, and when they had a problem, they would tell each other and help one another.

When the Sun saw what happened with the great water on the Earth, she called her friend and helper Bright Light.

"Oh, my friend," said the Sun, "I am so sad when I look down through the clouds onto the Mother Earth. Everything is wet and almost everything is dead. When the clouds are gone and the rain has stopped, there will not be much left. How will I ever be able to dry up all that water and still have enough strength left for the people and the animals and the plants, to make them strong and alive again?"

"Well, my dear Sun," said Bright Light, "I know I will help with all my strength, but I am not like you. My light will not reach down to the ground like your rays, yet there must be a way I can help."

They thought and thought, but they could not find a way. It took many days until Bright Light had an idea.

She went to the Sun and told her very happily, "I have a good idea to help you and Mother Earth. I will go down there myself with my light and warmth and help you, dear Sun."

"That is very kind of you," said the Sun, "but that will not be possible, because once you are down on Earth, there is no way you can come back to me."

Still her will and love to help was so strong that Bright Light could not be at rest.

The time came when the clouds went away and the Sun could start to dry up all the mountains and the ground. When the Good Creator saw all that nakedness, He was sad in His heart and went to the Sun.

"Dear Sun," said the Creator, "could you not help the plants grow faster? Some of the people and animals and birds will come back soon, and they will have nothing to eat. The ground is still so wet; nothing can grow."

"My dear Creator," answered the Sun, "I have worked very hard. I hardly have any strength left. I am so tired. I do my very best."

"Oh, yes, I know," said the Creator, "you have been very good, but . . . . "

At this moment Bright Light stood before the Creator, and with her soft voice she spoke.

"Oh Great Creator, let me go down to Earth," she pleaded. "My light and warmth cannot reach the Earth from here, but down there I can help my friend, the Sun."

The Creator saw how strong and great her love and will to help was, and He was very pleased.

"Well, He said, "that is very kind of you, but when you go down there, you cannot come back!"

"I know," said Bright Light, "but I still want to help. I am sure you will find a way for me. You know everything."

After a long while, the Creator spoke.

"I know what I shall do. I will give you a new life. I will change you into a very special and beautiful plant, a plant that will bring forth warmth and light into the day, a plant that will bear food for the people, the birds, and the animals."

"As you will not be able to come back here to the Sun," the Creator went on, "you shall be the tallest flower on Earth. You will always be nearer to the Sun than any other flower. I thank you for your love and kindness."

After these words, He transformed Bright Light into a seed. He carried her down to Earth and planted her into the ground and blessed her.

The seed grew into a strong plant and had a beautiful flower. She had a strong stem like a little tree, big leaves like the shape of a heart, and her flower looked like the Sun itself.

She did not stand there and enjoy her beauty, but with her strong roots she sucked up much water, and with her bright sun-like flower she radiated warmth and light to all around her.

Then the Creator put a rainbow into the sky to signal to all the people, and animals, and birds that there was new hope. When they saw this strong and beautiful flower, they were full of joy! They gave her the name she still has today; they called her "Sunflower."

The seeds, the leaves, and the roots gave them food and the people, birds, and animals did very well. It made the Sunflower so happy.

When you see a Sunflower today, have a good look at her. You will always find happiness. She is so happy that she can be of help to everyone.

Yet in her heart she longs to be back as Bright Light with her friend the Sun, and this is why she always turns her flower head towards the Sun from morning to evening until the Sun goes to sleep.

When you look at her good face in the morning, you will often find a few tears in it. So when you see a Sunflower, be good to her and tell her how much you love her, so that she doesn't feel so homesick.

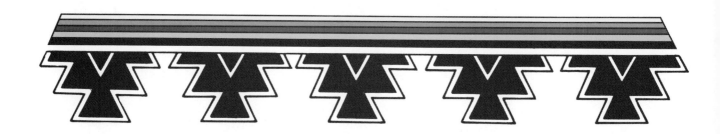

Walking Night Bear (Dr. Henryk Binder) has walked the Medicine Wheels of many nations. He has now returned to the Native American culture and tradition, and lives with his wife in British Columbia, Canada.

Stan Padilla is a Yaqui Indian artist and jewelry designer. He is the author and illustrator of the book *Dream Feather,* the story of a young Indian boy's spiritual awakening and mystical journey to the Sun. He is vitally interested and maintaining tradition among Native American young people. He lives and works with his family in northern California.